Seasons

Winter

Monica Hughes

www.raintreepublishers.co.uk

Visit our website to find out more information about **Raintree** books.

To order:
- ☎ Phone 44 (0) 1865 888112
- 🖹 Send a fax to 44 (0) 1865 314091
- 🖥 Visit the Raintree Bookshop at **www.raintreepublishers.co.uk** to browse our catalogue and order online.

First published in Great Britain by Raintree, Halley Court, Jordan Hill, Oxford OX2 8EJ, part of Harcourt Education.
Raintree is a registered trademark of Harcourt Education Ltd.

Editorial: Charlotte Guillain and Diyan Leake
Design: Michelle Lisseter
Picture Research: Maria Joannou and Liz Savery
Production: Lorraine Hicks

Originated by Dot Gradations
Printed and bound in China by
South China Printing Company

ISBN 1 844 21340 4 (hardback)
07 06 05 04
10 9 8 7 6 5 4 3 2

ISBN 1 844 21345 5 (paperback)
08 07 06 05 04
10 9 8 7 6 5 4 3 2 1

British Library Cataloguing in Publication Data
Hughes, Monica
Winter
508.2
A full catalogue record for this book is available from the British Library.

Acknowledgements
The publishers would like to thank the following for permission to reproduce photographs: Alamy Images pp. **18**, **23b**, **23c**; Alvey & Towers Sieve p. **23a**; Andy Purcell p. **7**; Bubbles pp. **6**, **8**, **9**, **23f**; Collections (Geoff Howard) p. **15**, **21**; FLPA (Catherine Mullen) p. **23d**; Garden Matters p. **23g**; Holt Studios International p. **12**; Jenny Bentley p. **14**; NHPA pp. **17**, **19**; Oxford Scientific Films p. **16**; RSPCA(Stephen Oliver) p. **23e**; Sally & Richard Greenhill pp. **10**, **11**; Simon Warner p. **13**; Still Moving Picture Company (Doug Corrance) p. **20**; Trevor Clifford p. **4**; Tudor Photography p. **22**; Woodfall Wild Images p. **5**.

Cover photograph of children playing in the snow, reproduced with permission of Getty Images/Stone.

Every effort has been made to contact copyright holders of any material reproduced in this book. Any omissions will be rectified in subsequent printings if notice is given to the publishers.

Contents

Some words are shown in bold, **like this**. You can find them in the glossary on page 23.

When is winter?

It is never clear when one season ends and the next one begins.

Winter is the season after autumn and before spring.

We say that winter starts on 21 December.

December, January and February are the winter months.

What is the weather like in winter?

It can be very cold in the winter even when the sun is shining.

There is **frost** and snow.

Cold winds can blow the snow into huge **drifts**.

Water freezes and turns into icicles.

What clothes do we wear in winter?

We need warm clothes in winter.

We wear strong shoes or boots and lots of **layers** of clothes.

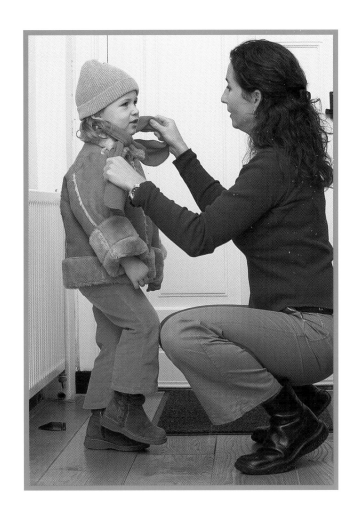

Hats, gloves and scarves give us extra protection against the cold.

What happens in towns in winter?

Roads and paths can be dangerous if they are covered in ice.

We need to clear roads to help prevent accidents.

Blizzards can cause problems for traffic, but snow is great fun to play in!

What happens in the country in winter?

Some animals are brought inside during the winter.

They will not go outside again until the weather gets warmer.

Animals living outside need
extra care.

What foods do we eat in winter?

We like warm food and hot drinks after being out in the cold.

Christmas is on 25 December.

There are lots of special foods at Christmas.

What happens to animals in winter?

Some animals curl up and **hibernate** during the winter months.

Other animals grow thick coats to protect them from the cold.

Birds fluff up their feathers to keep warm.

Food can be difficult to find.

What happens to plants in winter?

Many trees seem dead but **evergreen** trees look beautiful.

Very few plants grow during
the winter.

Jasmine and **snowdrops** are the few
flowers we can see in the winter.

What celebrations take place in winter?

People in Scotland welcome the New Year with music, singing and dancing.

This celebration is called Hogmanay.

At Chinese New Year there
are fireworks, decorations and
street parades.

Make a winter bird feeder

Attach some string to a fir cone.

Completely cover the cone with chunky peanut butter and dip it in birdseed.

Hang it up outside and watch the birds enjoy this tasty treat.

Glossary

blizzard
windy snow storm

drifts
piles of snow blown by the wind

evergreens
trees with leaves that stay green all year

frost
thin, powdery ice

hibernate
go into deep winter sleep

layers
when one thing lies on top of other things

snowdrop
a white flower that grows in the winter

Index

Titles in the Seasons series include:

Hardback   1 844 21337 4

Hardback   1 844 21338 2

Hardback   1 844 21339 0

Hardback   1 844 21340 4

Find out about the other titles in this series on our website www.raintreepublishers.co.uk